Keep this p ...ur you when
you are travelling around Norfolk.

Whether you are in your car or on foot, you will
enjoy an evocative journey back in time. Compare
the Norfolk of old with what you can see today
—see how the streets have changed, how shops and
buildings have been altered or replaced, how the
landscapes of the Broads have been developed; look
at fine details such as lamp-posts, shop fascias and
trade signs. See, too, the many alterations to the
Norfolk landscape that have taken place during our
lives, and which we may have taken for granted.

At the turn of a page you will gain fascinating
insights into Norfolk's unique history.

FRANCIS FRITH'S
pocket ALBUM

NORFOLK

A POCKET ALBUM

Adapted from an original book by
TERENCE SACKETT

FRITH
BOOK Co

First published in the United Kingdom in 2003 by
Frith Book Company Ltd

ISBN 1-85937-712-2

British Library Cataloguing in Publication Data

Norfolk—A Pocket Album
Adapted from an original book by Terence Sackett

Frith Book Company Ltd
Frith's Barn, Teffont,
Salisbury, Wiltshire SP3 5QP
Tel: +44 (0) 1722 716 376
Email: info@francisfrith.co.uk
www.francisfrith.co.uk

Printed and bound in Great Britain by MPG, Bodmin

Front Cover: Horning on the Broads 1902 / 48108 *The colour-tinting is for illustrative
purposes only, and is not intended to be historically accurate.*

Frontispiece: Coltishall, Horstead Mill 1902 / 48149

AS WITH ANY HISTORICAL DATABASE THE FRITH ARCHIVE IS CONSTANTLY
BEING CORRECTED AND IMPROVED AND THE PUBLISHERS WOULD
WELCOME INFORMATION ON OMISSIONS OR INACCURACIES

CONTENTS

FRANCIS FRITH
VICTORIAN PIONEER

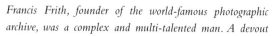

Francis Frith, founder of the world-famous photographic archive, was a complex and multi-talented man. A devout Quaker and a highly successful Victorian businessman, he was philosophic by nature and pioneering in outlook. By 1855 he had already established a wholesale grocery business in Liverpool, and sold it for the astonishing sum of £200,000, which is the equivalent today of over £15,000,000. Now in his thirties, and captivated by the new science of photography, Frith set out on a series of pioneering journeys up the Nile and to the Near East.

INTRIGUE AND EXPLORATION

He was the first photographer to venture beyond the sixth cataract of the Nile. Africa was still the mysterious 'Dark Continent', and Stanley and Livingstone's historic meeting was a decade into the future. The conditions for picture taking confound belief. He laboured for hours in his wicker dark-room in the sweltering heat of the desert, while the volatile chemicals fizzed dangerously in their trays. Back in London he exhibited his photographs and was 'rapturously cheered' by members of the Royal Society. His reputation as a photographer was made overnight.

VENTURE OF A LIFE-TIME

By the 1870s the railways had threaded their way across the country, and Bank Holidays and half-day Saturdays had been made obligatory by Act of Parliament. All of a sudden the working man and his family were able to enjoy days out, take holidays, and see a little more of the world.

With typical business acumen, Francis Frith foresaw that these new tourists would enjoy having souvenirs to commemorate their days out. For the next thirty years he travelled the country by train and by pony and trap, producing fine photographs of seaside resorts and beauty spots that were keenly bought by millions of Victorians. These prints were painstakingly pasted into family albums and pored over during the dark nights of winter, rekindling precious memories of summer excursions. Frith's studio was soon supplying retail shops all over the country, and by 1890 F Frith & Co had become the greatest specialist photographic publishing company in the world, with over 2,000 sales outlets, and pioneered the picture postcard.

FRANCIS FRITH'S LEGACY

Francis Frith had died in 1898 at his villa in Cannes, his great project still growing. The archive he created continued in business for another seventy years. By 1970 it contained over a third of a million pictures showing 7,000 British towns and villages.

Frith's legacy to us today is of immense significance and value, for the magnificent archive of evocative photographs he created provides a unique record of change in the cities, towns and villages throughout Britain over a century and more. Frith and his fellow studio photographers revisited locations many times down the years to update their views, compiling for us an enthralling and colourful pageant of British life and character.

We are fortunate that Frith was dedicated to recording the minutiae of everyday life. For it is this sheer wealth of visual data, the painstaking chronicle of changes in dress, transport, street layouts, buildings, housing, engineering and landscape that captivates us so much today, offering us a powerful link with the past and with the lives of our ancestors.

Computers have now made it possible for Frith's many thousands of images to be accessed almost instantly. The archive offers every one of us an opportunity to examine the places where we and our families have lived and worked down the years. Its images, depicting our shared past, are now bringing pleasure and enlightenment to millions around the world a century and more after his death.

NORFOLK
AN INTRODUCTION

Norfolk is made up of two distinct regions. Its first is a varied region of bare sandy heathlands in the west, marshlands and reedbeds in the east, and broad agricultural lands between, rolling along under expansive skies and studded with remote and picturesque villages. Its second more celebrated region is to be found at its margins, where a hundred miles of wind-blown coastline are swept by the relentless waves of the North Sea.

Though entirely separate in nature and character, these two countries are intimately joined by Norfolk's willow-fringed rivers, such as the Yare, Wensum and Thurne, which thread their way through its broad landscapes and wind past remote farms and villages. Through the county's long history these waterways have been vital carriers of agricultural produce and other goods for export to markets in Britain and overseas, and have opened the county up to the wider world.

Norfolk has a rich seafaring heritage. Since medieval times, its great harbours at King's Lynn and Yarmouth have been the haunt of fishermen following the herring and gathering the plentiful lobsters and shellfish in its quieter coastal waters. For many hundreds of years coastal trading vessels have wound their way down the county's waterways to offload freights from the Low Countries. Many of

ACLE

THE 17TH-CENTURY WINDMILL c1929 / A204048

Norfolk's ancient ports have long since silted-up and have discovered new roles as popular resort towns. Cromer, Sheringham, Wells and Hunstanton are now thronged with visitors in the summer months. Behind their crumbling cliffs are wide, solitary marshes, some now drained and cultivated, and rich in bird life.

Norfolk has been shaped to its core by the sea. For centuries, men have exercised their ingenuity in fending off the encroaching waters and reclaiming their fields and pastures. Where the dunes have been breached by tides the seas have flooded in. The old windmills that speckle Norfolk's rich, black marshlands, and the complex networks of dykes, bear testament to man's continual battle with nature. At the heart of the county are the Broads, unique shallow lagoons, shaped by the hands of medieval peat diggers, now the pleasure grounds of the county and the exclusive province of holiday and leisure craft.

Although it is a county of sparse population, Norfolk's towns and villages are rich in fine old buildings. The streets and market places of its market towns like East Dereham, Swaffham and Thetford reveal a pleasing harmony of flint and brick. King's Lynn, close by the Wash, is a treasure house of architectural gems. Norfolk's crowning glory, however, is the city of Norwich with its magnificent cathedral and winding streets of jettied houses.

Much of Norfolk has avoided the mechanisation found in other regions of Britain. It is still a county where the visitor can enjoy peace and solitude. It has long been a painter's paradise. Cotman and Crome have brought it renown, finding inspiration there for their celebrated water-colours, and transmuting its soft, liquid landscape tones into paint. Norfolk is a county that can still conjure the spirit of another age, away from the bustle and noise of the modern world.

HORNING

ON THE BROADS 1902 / 48108

This broad open space at the heart of the city is a kaleidoscope of noise and colour on market day. In the background is the soaring tower of the 15th-century 180ft long church of St Peter Mancroft, with its peal of twelve bells and concealed hammerbeam roof. Although motor cars have replaced the horses and carts, this 1929 view of the ancient Provision Market is, in essence, little changed from medieval days. The cries of the traders still echo above the sea of bright awnings, and handcarts still ply their trade amidst the throng.

NORWICH

MARKET PLACE 1929 / 81796

NORWICH

DAVEY PLACE 1922 / 72602

This busy prospect reveals the pleasing mix of architectural styles inevitable in any prosperous city. On the right is the old post office and the agricultural hall. Opposite is the Royal Hotel, with its red brick façade, steep roofs and decorative towers, promising Victorian travellers a sophisticated welcome.

NORWICH

THE ROYAL HOTEL & POST OFFICE 1901 / 46672

This beautiful 15th-century building overlooks the market place. From here the city has been governed since 1407. The glorious east-end, with its decorative chequerwork detailing, was completed in 1535. The ancient structure was once almost undermined by saltpetre diggers.

NORWICH

THE GUILDHALL 1891 / 28164

NORWICH

ELM HILL 1929 / 81805

This winding cobbled street, edged with handsome medieval timber-framed houses with flint-faced ground floors, was anciently known as Houndgate. A fire destroyed many of its buildings in 1507. It is hard to believe that it was scheduled for demolition earlier this century.

This massive medieval structure, formed of flint and ruddy Dutch bricks, squats close by the river, near Bishop Bridge. No one now knows why it was called 'Cow Tower', for in previous days it was the water toll gate where the monks' servants collected taxes on vessels plying the river. Traversed by a dozen bridges, the Wensum clutches the old city in a tight embrace. It was once a vital waterway for the carrying of fleeces and woollen produce, for Norwich was once one of the great weaving centres of medieval England.

NORWICH

OLD COW TOWER 1891 / 28158

NORWICH

BER STREET 1891 / 28162

*Ber Street leads the traveller out through the southern fringes
of the city. This quiet, shaded street offered a little respite
from the bustle of the market centre. The jumble of roof lines
reveals how city streets often developed piecemeal. On the
right is a fine display of baskets and tinware, although the
street was known at one time for its slaughter houses.*

THORPE-NEXT-NORWICH

THE RIVER YARE 1919 / 69075

John Sell Cotman, who founded the Norwich School of Artists with Crome, was born in this riverside village in 1782. The banks of the Yare are thick with chestnuts and willows, and pleasure boats and dinghies glide through smooth waters between fine old houses. Thorpe is now almost a suburb of Norwich. Further down is the Rush Cutters pub.

This pleasant market town sits on the road from Thetford to Norwich, and was once a resting place for pilgrims - it still has a Guild Chapel dedicated to St Thomas a Becket. The town is renowned for the number and quality of its historic houses, and is blessed with an ancient abbey, founded by William d'Albini in 1107. The fine half-timbered octagonal market cross, resting on timber stilts and stone arches, was built in 1605 after a fire destroyed a good proportion of the town. It has an outside wooden stair leading to a reading room.

WYMONDHAM

MARKET PLACE & CROSS c1965 / W159036

This lovely street, fringed with cobbles, leads down to the
White Lion Inn and the old church, where the poet William
Cowper, 'England's sweetest and most pious bard', was laid
to rest. On the left is Mr Kerrison the butcher's ornamented
shop front, with a refined iron balcony overhead.

EAST DEREHAM
CHURCH STREET 1893 / 33303

The Victorians were renowned for commemorating civic occasions in public architecture. In 1954, in similar fashion, the citizens of the town erected this imposing frieze across the roofs in memory of Withburga, daughter of one of the kings of the East Anglians. She established a nunnery at Dereham, and was laid to rest here in 654.

EAST DEREHAM

THE TOWN SIGN c1955 / D163100

A quiet lane on the fringes of the town. Washing dries in the breeze in the gardens of plain, mellow cottages. In the background are the two towers of St Nicholas's church. George Borrow, the 'gentleman gypsy', was lucky to have been born in this pleasing old country town. It enjoys a prosperity founded on more than its agricultural and market traditions—engineering works were established here in Victorian times and Dereham grew into one of the busiest centres of commerce in central Norfolk.

EAST DEREHAM

1893 / 33308

FAKENHAM

NORWICH STREET c1955 / F3002

Norwich Street reflects Fakenham's essential character. None of its brick buildings is outstanding yet the total effect is one of pleasing harmony. Many of the shops have retained their Victorian detailing. The postman, centre right, is delivering from his two-wheeled basket cart.

Some splendid Georgian brick buildings surround Fakenham's square. 18th-century architects, usually local men, worked from standard pattern books, yet managed to achieve townscapes of individual character and harmony.

FAKENHAM

THE WAR MEMORIAL 1921 / 71073

CASTLE ACRE

THE OLD GATE 1891 / 29111

Spanning the narrow street of this hill-top village, which rests high on the chalk uplands overlooking the River Nar, is this monumental arch, ancient gateway to the castle, which lies ruinous close by. Though castle and gateway were Norman-built, the settlement's origins are still more ancient, for it stands on the line of the Peddar Way, an ancient Celtic track.

SWAFFHAM

MARKET PLACE 1891 / 29104

This admirable market town, with its Queen Anne and Georgian buildings, was once hailed as 'the Montpellier of England'. Five roads meet at the broad market square. All around is a medley of harmonious red-brick. The church of St Peter and St Paul is a magnificent Perpendicular edifice with a grand hammerbeam roof and delicate spire.

Diss, this small, stylish town on the Suffolk border evolved around a six-acre pool called Diss Mere which penetrates almost to the edge of the main street. The town prospered in medieval times as a market for cloth and linen thread, which was spun and woven from local flax. The poet John Skelton was rector here for a quarter of a century. The spacious market place is dominated by the venerable flint church of St Mary's with its Norman tower, 14th-century arcades, impressive clerestory, and knapped flint chancel.

DISS

MARKET PLACE 1925 / 77322

DISS

MERE STREET 1925 / 77325

Mr Burden's shop and Post Office is the centre of village life. Here we see the local bobby returning to his beat—his cycle is parked under the signpost. On the wall is a bubble gum machine, once a popular feature of the frontage of every village store in the country. At the southern limits of the county, close by Diss, this delightful village of knapped flint cottages sits in wooded countryside in the valley of the Little Ouse.

GARBOLDISHAM

THE POST OFFICE c1955 / G188031

GARBOLDISHAM

HARVEST TIME c1955 / G188029

This photograph depicts a vanished way of life in the country. Horse-drawn wagons have brought in the straw from the fields. The rick-maker is at work—you can just spot a conical thatched roof in the background. Within a decade or two the roar of combine harvesters would mar the peaceful scene.

St Cuthbert's is a medieval church that was entirely rebuilt after its tower fell in 1851. On the right is the 1884 post office, with its decorative detailing, recalling the ancient East Anglian tradition of pargetting. Thetford enjoyed a high standing a millennium ago—during the 11th century it was the seat of the East Anglian bishopric. However, unlike the more northerly Norfolk towns, it never grew into a major centre of agriculture—the soils here are poor.

THETFORD

ST CUTHBERT'S CHURCH 1921 / 70915

The mill occupies an island between the two rivers, Thet and Little Ouse. In 1669 the course of the Little Ouse was cut and extended to Thetford, enabling barges to ply for the first time between the country towns of the region and the port of King's Lynn. By then, however, Lynn had already declined in status as a port, and Thetford never gained the prominence as a trading centre it expected.

THETFORD

MILL HEAD 1929 / 81834

In the market place is the Guildhall, rebuilt in 1900. Inside is a splendid collection of a hundred portraits of members of celebrated East Anglian families, which were bequeathed by the antiquary Prince Frederick Duleep Singh. It is market day, and the bystanders are waiting for transport to carry them back to their villages.

THETFORD

MARKET PLACE 1929 / 81830

This famous east coast resort has been a flourishing fishing port since the Conqueror's times. For centuries it suffered continual silting. By the 16th century the old river channel had become so blocked with sandbanks that the town burghers had to enlist the help of Dutch engineers to cut a new river mouth. The expansive market place has long been the commercial hub of the town. On market days it echoes Yarmouth's seafaring traditions, the colourful awnings stretching out like waves to the horizon. The glory of Yarmouth is its parish church of St Nicholas, the spire soaring high over the distant roofs. It was badly damaged by bombing in the Second World War.

GREAT YARMOUTH

THE MARKET 1891 / 28716

The imposing Queen Anne style Town Hall was built in 1882. The buildings clustering around this broad space, with their balconies, steep roofs and shutters, reveal a continental influence and reflect the town's cosmopolitan character—a legacy of its historic trading links with Europe.

GREAT YARMOUTH

TOWN HALL 1891 / G56501

GREAT YARMOUTH

BRITANNIA PIER 1904 / 52337

Many seaside piers began life as landing stages for pleasure steamers. Thrusting out into the sea they encapsulated the Victorian passion for exotic feats of engineering. Piers were soon the focus for holiday fun, where visitors could enjoy concerts or simply sit watching the crowds flow by. Britannia Pier was constructed in the mid 19th century, and is 810ft long.

Wellington Gardens is styled in the classical manner, with a domed bandstand reminiscent of St Paul's. Here the fashionable promenaded. The Winter Gardens to the left have been compared to a giant greenhouse where summer could be enjoyed the year long. The intention was clearly to create a holiday fantasy, worlds away from the grime and slog of city life. Beyond is the mid-Victorian Wellington Pier.

GREAT YARMOUTH

WELLINGTON GARDENS 1904 / 52338

Along Hall Quay are clustered craft of every kind: flat-bottomed barges, wherries and fishing boats—it is still the age of the sail. On the left is a line of coal wagons: Yarmouth had long been a colliers' and fishermens' port, and in its prime over 200 vessels were registered. Scots fisher girls followed the herring shoals down to the port in the autumn and worked tirelessly day and night gutting and packing.

GREAT YARMOUTH

TOWN HALL 1891 / 28699

GREAT YARMOUTH

THE BEACH 1887 / 19860

In this early view of the beach, there are already signs of local businesses capitalising on the new influx of visitors, with terraces of newly-built lodging houses and cheap hotels. A fleet of numbered pleasure craft is grouped on the sands. There are refreshments booths, gingerbread sellers, seats to rent by the hour, and donkey rides.

A peaceful scene away from the bustle of the front. In the hazy distance are the sails of boats. The street is lined with a medley of newly-constructed buildings. Victorian Yarmouth grew out of the efforts of individual speculators, with the consequence that there was no common plan or blueprint to ensure a harmonious townscape, as there would have been in Georgian times.

GREAT YARMOUTH

REGENT ROAD 1896 / 37959

GREAT YARMOUTH

ROW NUMBER 60 1908 / 60654

In this quintessential holiday scene a pleasure craft hoists its sail ready to carry a party of trippers up and down the coast. Children paddle in the shallows clutching their buckets and spades. In the background is one of Gorleston's many hotels, built to cater for the more well-heeled Edwardian visitor.

GORLESTON

THE BEACH 1904 / 52329

GORLESTON

THE SANDS 1896 / 37974

A lone tent sits on the empty sands. On the right is a bathing machine, which would be trundled down into the shallows by the patient horse so that lady bathers could dip their toes with no fear of prying eyes. Gorleston stands at the gateway of Yarmouth's harbour overlooking the River Yare and the sea. It had long been an old seafaring port but burgeoned into a sizeable town in the 19th century.

This solid structure, with its massive piles and defences, hints at the treacherous seas seafarers confronted off the Norfolk coast. An elegant lady shields her pale skin from the sun with a parasol. Beyond her, anglers cast their lines in expectation and a steamer prepares to berth at the quay.

GORLESTON

THE PIER 1904 / 52331

The awnings are still up on the bandstand and the musicians are tuning up in readiness for the afternoon matinee. A colourful throng is being entertained by pierrots on the beach. The women have dressed specially for the warm weather, but the men swelter in their workaday suits and hats—the Edwardian tourists had no special holiday outfits as we do today. Gorleston's pavilion was built in 1898.

The fishing fleet, having waited patiently for a breeze, can at last set sail in pursuit of the herring. In the heyday of the industry the quays would have been thronged with fisher girls gutting the catch. Little more than a decade later most of the sailing barges had been replaced by modern steam-driven vessels.

GORLESTON

THE HARBOUR 1894 / 33393

HOPTON

THE HOLIDAY CAMP c1955 / H310084

Hopton is a diminutive village resort on the A12 just south of Great Yarmouth. Here holiday makers could enjoy the quiet attractions of the 'Constitutional Holiday Camp' well away from the bustle and bright lights of its noisier and bigger neighbour. Every effort has been made to intensify the holiday atmosphere: there are 'cabin' style chalets daubed with bright colours, rustic seats, flower-bedded lawns and plenty of beach space.

Although there are many pleasant cottages in the vernacular brick and flint, the modest village street does not reflect Caister's illustrious history. Caister's Castle was built by Sir John Fastolf when he returned from the French wars. Having led the English archers at Agincourt, he was seeking well-deserved repose and retirement. The castle later passed to the Paston family, its chequered history described in their famous letters.

CAISTER ON SEA

HIGH STREET c1955 / C450078

For many working people life after the War was gray and utilitarian. Holiday camps like Caister's offered inexpensive breaks for the whole family - with all costs included. The chalets were spartan, but there was the certainty of meeting new friends as well as a plethora of free activities. A good time was assured for all. The family tricycle was always a popular attraction.

CAISTER ON SEA

THE HOLIDAY CAMP c1955 / C450025

The Broads have been a watery playground for holidaymakers for decades. It is hard to believe that these broad expanses of smooth water are man-made. In medieval times peat was dug on a grand scale and the landscape would have appeared very different. The diggings were originally dry, resembling great open-cast mines, and were prone to flooding and inundation during times of rising water levels. This placid scene depicts the Broads as every water traveller would wish to experience them. There is no jostling, no locks nor congested passages, only a broad silent water fringed with reed beds and a fine, picturesque windmill.

THE BROADS

MILL AND RIVER c1934 / T213064

Sunset against sombre skies, dark shadowy trees, an invisible breeze, the slap of waters among the reeds ... a woman in pinafore dress and bonnet punts her way home after the day's toil. This atmospheric scene captures the essential spirit of the Broads with their silent, solitary backwaters.

THE BROADS

THE EVENING FERRY C1900 / T213073

ACLE

As one old guide book pointed out, 'To every broadsman who quants his wherry along the slow rivers, Acle Bridge is a haven or port of call. Many are the little ships of adventure which lower their masts and sails to pass beneath'. The early Victorian bridge was once the scene of more dubious activities—criminals were executed here by being hanged from the parapet.

Horning is blessed with a wealth of reed-thatched cottages with eye-browed dormers, as well as other more unusual buildings—the house alongside where the car is parked has crow-stepped gables, revealing a Dutch influence. Horning is fortunate to have retained much of its Edwardian charm, unlike its brasher, more commercial neighbours.

HORNING

THE VILLAGE 1934 / 86364

This charming village straddles the banks of the River Bure amidst beautiful marshland. Set in the heart of Broadland, it has been called 'little Venice', with soft green lawns spreading down to the water's edge. In the summer months it is thronged with pleasure boats, and all is bustle and noise. Here village policemen are directing the summer traffic.

HORNING

THE VILLAGE 1934 / 86365

Broadland is strewn with relics of previous ages. Here an old wind pump, its sails still set against the breeze, takes on the character of a living tree with its roughly-hewn timber supports. Such pumps were vital to help drainage on wet lands and were in use right up until the middle of the 20th century.

HORNING

AN OLD WIND PUMP 1902 / 48110

HORNING

Amidst the Cowholm marshes are the scanty ruins of St Benet's Abbey, founded by Canute. It has the reputation of being the only abbey not dissolved at the Dissolution, its revenues continuing to provide an income for the Bishop of Norwich. Within its bounds a marshland drainage mill was built many years ago, its smooth, conical form combining curiously with the jagged broken masonry of the old gatehouse.

HOVETON

THE VILLAGE 1921 / 70890

At Hoveton there is a full mile of shimmering open water which is thronged with pleasure craft in the summer months. A street trader has pushed his hand cart into the middle of the street and nonchalantly weighs out vegetables regardless of passing traffic. He must make the most of his monopoly: a competitor, his cart overladen with trays of vegetables, is hurrying towards the junction.

Three decades later, the quiet cross ways of the previous view present a
very different character. Roy's, 'the biggest village shop in the world' has
plumped itself over two corners. The proprietors are keen to get their
hands on the visitors' holiday money: there are signs for chocolate, cards,
Kodak film, millinery, soft drinks, toilet requisites … and in the far
distance hoardings advertise trips on the Broads, Judges postcards, guides
and maps, Goss china and newspapers.

HOVETON

THE VILLAGE c1950 / H399112

A mile from Wroxham Broad and spanning the Bure is this lovely old single-span bridge, partially hidden by a passing sail. Gardens slope down to the river, and thick canopies of trees at the water's edge keep the wind from the sails of boats. The banks of the Bure here are pitted with artificial basins, where boats lie up in safety during the long months of winter.

WROXHAM

ON THE BURE 1921 / 70893

COLTISHALL

A CORNFIELD 1902 / 48127

*Horses graze the rich meadows that keep the waters
of the River Bure from the village street. Handsome
pantile-roofed red-brick houses line the grassy banks.
A rotted hulk squats in a narrow inlet. To the left of
the picture are shallow-roofed warehouses.*

COLTISHALL

THE VILLAGE 1902 / 48166

The 'Widgeon' is drawn up alongside the mill offloading its cargo. Fully laden, such wherries would only draw a little over two feet, making them the perfect vessels for navigating the shallow waters of the Broads. Note the single high-peaked mainsail, its considerable height allowing the craft to collect every last puff of wind that passed over the thick canopy of trees fringing the banks.

COLTISHALL

HORSTEAD MILL 1902 / 48150

An old boatman with a bright neckerchief sits on his oars, having rowed a passenger to this quiet backwater amongst the reedbeds. She stands at the water's edge enjoying the birdsong and the vistas of open water. It is late afternoon and at last there are long, cool shadows to refresh the weary.

COLTISHALL

THE RIVER 1902 / 48159

Much of this prosperous market town, north of the Broads, was rebuilt after a major fire in 1600. Its pleasing Georgian facades spread round the market place. North Walsham was once a significant weaving centre. Its prosperity was increased after a canal was dug connecting the River Ant with the Broads.

NORTH WALSHAM

MARKET PLACE 1921 / 70936

Ludham sits on 'high' ground, which in Broadland can be just a few feet above sea level. The flat lands around are threaded by three great rivers, the Thurne, Ant and Bure. The old wind pump at Turf Fen, its sails now still, offers testament to man's battle with the rising flood waters down the centuries.

LUDHAM

THE OLD WIND PUMP C1955 / L110082

POTTER HEIGHAM

THE BRIDGE 1934 / 86381

The old medieval stone bridge, with one central and two pointed side arches, carries Yarmouth-bound traffic over the Thurne. Its painted warning 'Caution, proceed slowly' must not be ignored. Generations ago, even the great trading wherries had to halt and drop their masts to gain passage. Today the village is mainly the province of pleasure craft, who clog the quays in the months of summer.

*At Hickling, where the Broadland waters fan into expansive shallows,
there is a pleasing jumble of red tiled and thatched buildings clustering
around the old Pleasure Boat Inn. John of Oxnead, a monk at nearby
St Benet's Abbey, recounts how, in 1287, the sea burst in upon the flat
shorelands and the town of 'Hyckelnygge'.*

HICKLING

THE PLEASURE BOAT INN c1955 / H307011

This tiny settlement is set in a remote area of the Broads, where willows and reed beds thrust out into the waters narrowing the passage. It looks peaceful enough, but it is just two miles from the coast, and down by the dunes the sea blows unrelentingly. On many unforgettable nights at high tide, angry seas have broken through the banks and flooded thousands of acres of farmland.

HORSEY

THE MERE c1955 / H341009

CROMER

THE SANDS 1899 / 44482

Set high above the sea, but sheltered by wooded hills, Cromer was once was little more than a jumble of simple cottages huddled around the church, and the exclusive haunt of fishermen and crabbers. The town burgeoned into a popular resort with the coming of the railways. Only Yarmouth attracts more visitors.

It can be a long dangerous slide down the tiered sea walls to the sands and pier. The smart new flight of steps allowed ladies in long dresses to make a dignified descent. One Edwardian visitor recalls an excursion to Cromer in a wagon lent by a local farmer. He sent a postcard to his mother to let her know he had arrived safely. It was delivered by the afternoon post the same day!

CROMER

FROM THE WEST 1906 / 56850

CROMER

THE PIER 1902 / 49062

Cromer's 500ft-long pier was built in 1901 to replace a landing jetty destroyed by gales in 1897. In the storms of 1953 it was damaged again. A young woman stands with her grandmother a little along from the Bath Hotel. They encapsulate the fundamental changes in fashion that occurred during the first years of our century—the older woman must be sweltering in her dark, burdensome Victorian gown.

The beach was the centre of fun and frivolity. The flags are flying and a throng of holidaymakers waits to board a fleet of row boats for a trip along the coast. Though Cromer crabs were famous and plentiful, the Cromer fishermen welcomed the opportunity to make a few extra shillings from the summer trade with their boats.

CROMER

THE SANDS 1899 / 44485

Cromer's lifeboatmen are renowned for their gallantry. Henry Blogg, coxswain of the 'Louisa Heartwell', pictured here, was the most decorated lifeboatman in Britain, earning three gold and four silver medals, the George Cross and the British Empire medal for his bravery. Most of the Cromer rescues were carried out on the treacherous Haisboro' Sands.

CROMER

THE LIFEBOAT 1922 / 72651

A young lad sits on the grass on the sheltered inward side of the cliffs. The new lighthouse perches on the most prominent point, its powerful beam sweeping nightly across the dark sky and spilling its light over the walls of the parish church like a searchlight. The church itself was once used as a sea mark by mariners.

CROMER

THE LIGHTHOUSE 1894 / 33325

EAST RUNTON

HIGH STREET 1921 / 70970

East Runton offered visitors the same spectacular cliff scenery and ample beaches as its close neighbour, Cromer, but less of the noise and bustle. The Edwardian terraces in the foreground, with their bay windows and neat, walled gardens and railings, harmonise with the simpler cottages beyond.

Poorly compacted, and composed of glacial drift, the cliffs of the north Norfolk coast have been compared to 'dirty tallow', being unstable and liable to erosion. A row of white beach huts trims the foot of the cliffs like a cuff. In the distance is Cromer pier.

EAST RUNTON

LOOKING EAST 1933 / 85828

The town comprises two villages, Upper and Lower Sheringham, the former more peaceful and retaining its fishing and farming traditions. Some of the High Street shops and houses reveal a Dutch influence, with mansard roofs and ornamental gables. The blinds are down, it is a hot day. Developments away from exclusive local suppliers in retailing are already apparent, with Lincoln's offering 'choicest New Zealand mutton, fresh every morning'.

SHERINGHAM
HIGH STREET 1901 / 46544

SHERINGHAM

THE BEACH 1893 / 33311

*A typically ramshackle fishermen's scene, with boats drawn up on the
shingle, which is littered with maritime paraphernalia. As tourism
expanded, and smart visitors arrived in ever greater numbers, such
untidiness was frowned on by local businesses—the town had to smarten
up its image.*

Noble trees cluster round the churchyard wall. To the left is the
public drinking fountain, decorated with embedded pebbles, which
was constructed in the 1820s. The lane is plain compacted mud.
In winter it would be treacherous. To the south of the town is
remote heath and woodland.

SHERINGHAM

THE CHURCH 1894 / 33316

SHERINGHAM

FISHERMEN 1893 / 33313

Sheringham fishermen pursued not only crabs and lobsters but herring, cod and whiting. They were the traditional enemies of Cromer men, who referred to them disparagingly as 'Shaddocks'. Nets were regularly cut and battles fought. However, with their hats set at a rakish angle, these impressive Sheringham fishermen look formidable adversaries.

Sheringham fishermen gather round a lobster boat for the camera. They ventured out in open boats in all weathers. Fishing was a rough and dangerous way to earn a living. The North Sea tides could prove fatal for small craft, and more than once the Cromer lifeboat was forced out into bad weather to rescue whelkers. These men are suitably dressed for foul conditions in their thigh-length sea boots and thick fishermen's ganseys.

SHERINGHAM

THE BEACH 1901 / 46540

CLEY-NEXT-THE-SEA

THE WINDMILL 1933 / 85836

*This picturesque flint village was once the most significant of
the Glaven estuary ports, and its old Custom House bears
testimony to its prestigious past. Silting of the waterway
presaged the decline of Cley's influence, and coastal vessels
now pass it by. The fine old windmill dates from 1713, and
guards the town from the open marshlands.*

Standing on the fringes of the Norfolk marshes, Blakeney like Cley, once knew busier days. Its capacious natural harbour, protected from the sea by the long spit of sand, Blakeney Point, attracted coastal trading vessels until the early years of this century. The landscape offers bird-watchers an irresistible mixture of dunes, saltings, mud-flats and creeks.

BLAKENEY

THE REGATTA c1955 / B121087

The town is studded with fine brick and flint houses with steep pantiled roofs—on the right is the flamboyant brick and pebble Barclay's Bank. Hayward's the confectioner and newsagent, on the left, has retained its attractive wooden facia and ornamental painted signboard.

BLAKENEY

POST OFFICE CORNER c1955 / B121025

WELLS-NEXT-THE-SEA

1929 / 81996

From Wells to Blakeney, a great sand barrier holds back all but the most vicious tides. The quay at Wells is now stranded a mile from the open sea. The harbour was developed by the railway companies—wagons of the London Midland Scottish Line are drawn up at the quayside. In the background is a medley of vintage buildings, some with crow-stepped gables characteristic of the Low Countries, reflecting the town's historic trading links.

The Wells whelkers are renowned along this coast for their persistence in pursuing their trade. Whelking was not always a comfortable affair. Dropping pots from open clinker-built boats in pitch darkness and foul weather meant the Wells whelkers could often find themselves stranded for hours on end on the wrong side of the bar waiting for the tide.

WELLS-NEXT-THE-SEA

THE QUAY 1929 / 81998

WELLS-NEXT-THE-SEA

THE QUAY c1955 / W48061

The limitless flat salt marshes stretch out beyond the narrow channel. These heavily-laden fishermen use shoulder yokes to carry their shellfish, much as a milkmaid carries her buckets, paddling out of the shallows from their open boats, the 'Nell' and 'Armistice'. A few modest coastal vessels still unload here but Wells has now given itself over to more lucrative summer tourism.

WELLS-NEXT-THE-SEA

BRINGING IN THE COCKLES 1929 / 82003

Fisher's store is selling Raleigh, Rudge and Humber cycles. To its right is a fish and chip shop, which must rely on a good degree of passing trade. The 'Black Boys', with its multi-paned windows and pantiled roof, is a classic village inn, small and intimate.

ALDBOROUGH

THE BLACK BOYS c1955 / A278003

Holt, between Fakenham and Cromer, boasts a wealth of fine Georgian houses, which huddle haphazardly around its broad market place. It was rebuilt all of a piece after a devastating fire in 1708. On the left is a fine Victorian shopfront imposed on a plain brick house. The town is renowned for its public school, Gresham's, founded in 1555 by John Gresham, Lord Mayor of London.

HOLT

HIGH STREET 1896 / 37976

The shop on the extreme right has an imposing pavement display of bamboo baskets, chairs and hatstands, and a wide variety of galvanised tinware. It also reveals a somewhat insensitive example of infill, no attempt having been made by the architect to follow the existing roof line.

HOLT

MARKET PLACE 1896 / 37977

WALSINGHAM

SHEEP GOING TO MARKET 1929 / 82040

Walsingham is built around the ruins of a monastic house, celebrated for its shrine to Our Lady of Walsingham. It is an important place of pilgrimage, second only to Becket's tomb at Canterbury. Fringed by rich woodland, and with a medieval well, priory and many splendid timber-framed houses, Walsingham retains a powerful historic and religious atmosphere for visitors. This old shepherd, plodding on to Walsingham market, has been enjoying a glass of ale in the 'White Hart'.

WALSINGHAM

THE PRIORY GATEWAY 1922 / 72628

Hunstanton is unique for north Norfolk resort towns in that it looks west across the sea and not east. It was a quiet village of simple fishermen's cottages until the coming of the railway in 1862. Then building began in earnest as visitors flocked to enjoy its safe, sandy beach and bracing cliff-top walks. The new town is gathered around an expansive green.

HUNSTANTON

THE GREEN 1901 / 47641

HUNSTANTON

THE GREEN 1907 / 58895

Genteel and intimate, Hunstanton attracted the more discerning visitor.
Here, middle class children enjoy a game of cricket. The Great Eastern
Railway Company Hotel stands in the background. Hunstanton grew out
of the hamlet of Hunstanton St Edmund, sited low on the cliffs and owned
by the Le Strange family of the Hall. They saw its potential as a popular
resort, and soon prestigious hotels were clothing the edges of the green.

Hunstanton's lighthouse was built in 1830, and crowns the chalk clifftop close by the ruins of St Edmund's chapel, where pilgrims offered their prayers and sought the healing powers of the town's efficacious springs. Legend has it that Edmund, before becoming king of East Anglia, was almost shipwrecked here in treacherous seas, and founded the chapel in gratitude to God for sparing his life.

HUNSTANTON

THE LIGHTHOUSE 1891 / 28773

HEACHAM

HIGH STREET c1955 / H57084

This small village sits between the sea and fields of bright lavender. At Caley Mill there is a lavender water distillery, and in late summer the fields shimmer with a deep blue. The railway from Heacham to Wells was a lifeline for the export of local grain, vegetables, bricks and shellfish for metropolitan markets.

This illustrious and sublime town is on the east bank of the River Ouse, two miles from the Wash. Silting of the Ouse's ponderous waters robbed the town of much of its former prestige as a seaport, but its many graceful buildings and old Custom House have brought to it the appellation of 'most romantic town in England'. Cargoes of wool, cloth from Flanders, and timber from the Baltic crossed into England here. Friars Fleet winds along the back of King's Lynn and joins the River Ouse close by the quay. Southgate is a remnant of the old town walls.

KING'S LYNN

SOUTHGATE 1891 / 28760

113

KING'S LYNN

HIGH STREET 1908 / 60024

This street of small distinctive shops and fine 18th-century terraced buildings is the commercial hub of the town. Spanning the street are a pair of open decorative iron arches on which are hung the town lamps. On the left is a formidable display of boots and shoes cascading over the shop facia.

Lynn's market place is one of the very finest in England, enriched by a profusion of Georgian and Victorian public buildings, including the florid Corn Exchange built in 1854. This scene would have changed little over many hundreds of years: farmers' wives travelled in by pony and trap to sell fresh fruit and vegetables, and market traders shouted for business from below colourful awnings.

KING'S LYNN

THE TUESDAY MARKET 1898 / 40886

KING'S LYNN

HIGH STREET 1908 / 60023

Jermyn and Perry's considerable premises dominate this busy High Street scene. Their display is spectacular, with hats, parasols, curtains and bolts of cloth tumbling out on to the pavement in a visual feast. It would surely have required a staff of full-time window-dressers to keep up. The business was later taken over by Debenham's.

The Purfleet, with its low bridge, is an old tidal inlet of the Ouse. Here stands the exquisite Custom House of 1683, with its graceful classical-style facade. It began life as the Merchants' Exchange, with an open-arched arcade on the ground floor. This was blocked in 1718 when the building was converted for use as a Customs House.

KING'S LYNN

THE CUSTOM HOUSE 1898 / 40878

KING'S LYNN

THE TOWN HALL AND GUILDHALL 1891 / 28754

This magnificent tour de force of flint and stone chequerwork was built in 1421 for the Guild of Holy Trinity, a wealthy group of merchants. Above the many-mullioned rectangular window of the porch are the arms of Edward the Sixth and Elizabeth. Many civic treasures are held within, including the Red Book of Lynn, in which are recorded the municipal records from 1204 to 1392. The matching town hall was built in 1895.

DOWNHAM MARKET

THE CLOCK TOWER c1950 / D149010

Like so many of its neighbours, Downham Market was a river port of some importance until railway workings cut it off from the waters of the Ouse. Perched on high ground at the fringes of the Fens, it is a town that conceals its long history—rich finds of Romano-British pottery confirm that it was a considerable settlement in Roman times, with peat being dug in huge quantities. The town presents a mellow and harmonious face to the visitor.

DOWNHAM MARKET

HIGH STREET C1950 / D149011

INDEX

PLEASE HELP US BRING FRITH'S PHOTOGRAPHS TO LIFE

Our authors do their best to recount the history of the places they write about. They give insights into how particular towns and villages developed, they describe the architecture of streets and buildings, and they discuss the lives of famous people who lived there. But however knowledgeable our authors are, the story they tell is necessarily incomplete.

Frith's photographs are so much more than plain historical documents. They are living proofs of the flow of human life down the generations. They show real people at real moments in history; and each of those people is the son or daughter of someone, the brother or sister, aunt or uncle, grandfather or grandmother of someone else. All of them lived, worked and played in the streets depicted in Frith's photographs.

We would be grateful if you would tell us about the many places shown in our photographs—the streets with their buildings, shops, businesses and industries. Describe your own memories of life in those streets: what it was like growing up there, who ran the local shop and what shopping was like years ago; if your workplace is shown tell us about your working day and what the building is used for now. With your help more and more Frith photographs can be brought to life, and vital memories preserved for posterity.

We will gradually add your comments and stories to the archive for the benefit of historians of the future. Wherever possible, we will try to include some of your comments in future editions of our books. Moreover, if you spot errors in dates, titles or other facts, please let us know, because our archive records are not always completely accurate—they rely on 150 years of human endeavour and hand-compiled records.

So please write, fax or email us with your stories and memories. Thank you!

CHOOSE ANY PHOTOGRAPH FROM THIS BOOK

for your FREE Mounted Print. Order further prints at half price

Fill in and cut out the voucher on the next page and return it with your remittance for £2.50 for postage, packing and handling to UK addresses (US $5.00 for USA and Canada). For all other overseas addresses include £5.00 post and handling.
Choose any photograph included in this book. Make sure you quote its unique reference number eg. 42365 (it is mentioned after the photograph date. 1890 / 42365). Your SEPIA print will be approx 12" x 8" and mounted in a cream mount with a burgundy rule line (overall size 14" x 11").

Mounted Print
Overall size 14 x 11 inches

Order additional Mounted Prints at HALF PRICE - If you would like to order more Frith prints from this book, possibly as gifts for friends and family, you can buy them at half price (with no extra postage and handling costs) - only £7.49 each (UK orders), US $14.99 each (USA and Canada).

---

* IMPORTANT!

These special prices are only available if you order at the same time as you order your free mounted print. You must use the ORIGINAL VOUCHER on the facing page (no copies permitted). We can only despatch to one address.

Have your Mounted Prints framed (UK orders only) - For an extra £14.95 per print you can have your mounted print(s) framed in an elegant polished wood and gilt moulding, overall size 16" x 13" (no additional postage).

FRITH PRODUCTS AND SERVICES

All Frith photographs are available for you to buy as framed or mounted prints. From time to time, other illustrated items such as Address Books, Calendars, Table Mats are also available. Already, almost 50,000 Frith archive photographs can be viewed and purchased on the internet through the Frith website.

For more detailed information on Frith companies and products, visit

www.francisfrith.co.uk

For further information, trade, or author enquiries, contact:

The Francis Frith Collection, Frith's Barn, Teffont, Salisbury SP3 5QP
Tel: +44 (0) 1722 716 376 Fax: +44 (0) 1722 716 881 Email: sales@francisfrith.co.uk

Voucher

for FREE
and Reduced Price
Frith Prints

Do not photocopy this voucher. Only the original is valid, so please fill it in, cut it out and return it to us with your order.

Picture ref no	Page number	Qty	Mounted @ £7.49 UK @$14.99 US	Framed + £14.95 (UK only)	US orders Total $	UK orders Total £
1		1	Free of charge*	£	$	£
2			£7.49 ($14.99)	£	$	£
3			£7.49 ($14.99)	£	$	£
4			£7.49 ($14.99)	£	$	£
5			£7.49 ($14.99)	£	$	£
			£7.49 ($14.99)	£	$	£

Please allow 28 days for delivery	* Post & handling	$5.00	£2.50
	Total Order Cost US $		£

Title of this book . . . .

I enclose a cheque / postal order (UK) for £ . . . . $ . . . .
payable to 'Francis Frith Collection' (USA orders 'Frith USA Inc')

OR debit my Mastercard / Visa / Switch (UK) / Amex card / Discover (USA)
(credit cards only on non UK and US orders), card details below

Card Number

Issue No (Switch only)   Valid from (Amex/Switch)

Expires   Signature

Name Mr/Mrs/Ms . . . .
Address . . . .
. . . .
. . . .
Postcode/Zip. . . . . Country . . . .
Daytime Tel No . . . .   Valid to 31/12/06

PAYMENT CURRENCY: We only accept payment in £ Sterling or US $.
If you are ordering **from any other country, please pay by credit card,** and you will be charged in one of these currencies.